Henry A. (Henry Augustus) Boardman

The American Union

A Discourse Delivered on Thursday, December 12, 1850

Henry A. (Henry Augustus) Boardman

The American Union
A Discourse Delivered on Thursday, December 12, 1850

ISBN/EAN: 9783337008390

Printed in Europe, USA, Canada, Australia, Japan

Cover: Foto ©Suzi / pixelio.de

More available books at **www.hansebooks.com**

THE

AMERICAN UNION:

A DISCOURSE

DELIVERED ON THURSDAY, DECEMBER 12, 1850,

THE DAY OF THE ANNUAL THANKSGIVING IN PENNSYLVANIA,

AND REPEATED ON THURSDAY, DECEMBER 19,

IN THE TENTH PRESBYTERIAN CHURCH, PHILADELPHIA.

BY
HENRY A. BOARDMAN, D. D.

Fourth Thousand.

PHILADELPHIA:
LIPPINCOTT, GRAMBO AND CO.,
SUCCESSORS TO GRIGG, ELLIOT & CO.
1851.

To the Rev. HENRY A. BOARDMAN, D. D.

PHILADELPHIA, *December* 20*th*, 1850.

DEAR SIR:—Your friends and immediate fellow-citizens who have listened to your discourse on the Union, are naturally desirous of sharing with the country at large the advantages of so valuable a production.

The spirit of true patriotism which it breathes is especially calculated to do good by being widely diffused at the present moment, while it is distinguished by a tone of piety that is auspicious at all times, and cannot fail to be universally acceptable.

In the name of all who had the satisfaction to witness your eloquence on this interesting occasion, we respectfully ask that you would favor us with the use of the manuscript for publication.

With sincere respect and regard,
Your friends and faithful servants,

J. R. INGERSOLL,	G. M. DALLAS,
R. PATTERSON,	W. M. MEREDITH,
JOHN K. FINDLAY,	JOS. PATTERSON,
W. C. PATTERSON,	R. M. PATTERSON,
JOHN W. FORNEY,	EDWARD ARMSTRONG,

JOHN S. RIDDLE.

———

PHILADELPHIA, *December* 20*th*, 1850.
To the Rev. HENRY A. BOARDMAN, D. D.

REVEREND AND DEAR SIR:—Cordially approving the sentiments expressed by you in your recent discourse on the AMERICAN UNION, and believing that a more general diffusion of these sentiments would tend to the formation of a sound public opinion on this very important subject, and being desirous, moreover, individually, in some explicit and formal manner, to testify our own devout attachment to the Union, and our utter dissent from those who would subvert it, and our determination to abide by the Constitution and laws, and more particularly those laws of the last session of Congress known as the Compromise Acts, we, the undersigned, do most gratefully and heartily thank you for your eloquent and timely discourse on this subject, and request a copy of the same for publication.

ALEX. W. MITCHELL, M. D.,	CHARLES B. PENROSE,
WM. H. DILLINGHAM,	A. V. PARSONS,
LAWRENCE LEWIS,	JOHN S. HART,
WM. SHIPPEN, M. D.,	JAMES B. ROGERS,
C. B. JAUDON,	WM. HARRIS, M. D.
HUGH ELLIOT,	J. N. DICKSON,
FRANCIS WEST, M. D.,	SMITH, MURPHY & Co.,
WM. GOODRICH,	HOGAN & THOMPSON,
R. R. BEARDEN,	J. B. ROSS,
TURNER, HARRIS & HALE,	JAMES BOGGS,
JAMES IMBRIE, JR.,	LIPPINCOTT, GRAMBO & Co.,

Jno. R. Vogdes,
John K. Townsend, M. D.,
W. II. Gillingham, M. D.,
A. B. Cummings,
John H. Brown,
Samuel Hood,
William B. Hieskell,
Moses Johnson,
Dale, Ross & Withers,
Thos. H. Hoge,
Dundas T. Pratt,
F. N. Buck,
James Orne,
James Schott,
Wm. Veitch,
Lind & Brother,
Taylor & Paulding,
B. P. Hutchinson,
Sibley, Moulton & Woodruff,
David Springs & Co.,
R. B. Brinton & Co.,
James Leslie,

Peter L. Ferguson,
Truitt, Brother & Co.,
Martin & Smith,
W. Kirk,
Arthur A. Burt,
Morris Patterson,
Faust & Winebrenner,
William Brown,
D. B. Birney,
Gemmill & Cresswell,
J. G. Mitchell,
Scott, Baker & Co.,
J. Anspach, Jr.,
Geo. C. Barber,
J. W. Tilford,
Jno. McArthur,
Robt. M. Slaymaker,
A. W. Slack,
James Burrowes,
Knorr & Fuller,
De Coursey, Lafourcade & Co.,
Maurice A. Wurts,

Henry R. Davis.

Philadelphia, *December* 23d, 1850.

Gentlemen:—I cannot doubt that the favor with which my late humble effort in behalf of the Union has been received, is to be ascribed more to the existing state of the public mind on this subject, than to the intrinsic merits of the performance itself. I do not feel at liberty, however, to decline an application emanating from a body of my fellow-citizens so honorably representing the commerce of our city, and the learned professions, and comprising gentlemen whose public services have won for them the respect and gratitude of the nation, and identified their fame with that of the Union.

In the hope that the discourse which you have in such flattering terms requested for publication may be made, by a good Providence, instrumental in promoting in some degree the cause which we all have so much at heart, I herewith place the manuscript at your disposal.

I am very faithfully,

Your friend and fellow-citizen,

H. A. BOARDMAN.

To the Hon. Joseph R. Ingersoll,
Major-General Patterson,
Hon. George M. Dallas,
Hon. Wm. M. Meredith,
Hon. Charles B. Penrose,
Hon. A. V. Parsons,
Alex. W. Mitchell, M. D.
Wm. H. Dillingham, Esq.,
Professor Hart,
Lawrence Lewis, Esq., and others.

THE UNION.

Do ye thus requite the LORD, O foolish people and unwise? *is* not he thy father *that* hath bought thee? hath he not made thee, and established thee?

Remember the days of old, consider the years of many generations: ask thy father, and he will show thee; thy elders, and they will tell thee.

When the Most High divided to the nations their inheritance, when he separated the sons of Adam, he set the bounds of the people according to the number of the children of Israel.

For the LORD's portion *is* his people; Jacob *is* the lot of his inheritance.

He found him in a desert land, and in the waste howling wilderness; he led him about, he instructed him, he kept him as the apple of his eye.

As an eagle stirreth up her nest, fluttereth over her young, spreadeth abroad her wings, taketh them, beareth them on her wings;

So the LORD alone did lead him, and *there was* no strange god with him.

He made him ride on the high places of the earth, that he might eat the increase of the fields; and he made him to suck honey out of the rock, and oil out of the flinty rock;

Butter of kine, and milk of sheep, with fat of lambs, and rams of the breed of Bashan, and goats, with the fat of kidneys of wheat; and thou didst drink the pure blood of the grape.—DEUT. XXXII. 6—14.

THESE words delineate with great beauty of imagery the general course of the Divine dispensations towards ancient Israel. Susceptible as they are of a ready adaptation to our own country, they suggest some of the various causes for gratitude to the Supreme Disposer of events, which should animate our hearts

2

as we assemble in our sanctuaries on this DAY OF
THANKSGIVING. But they also intimate (if we choose
thus to appropriate the passage to ourselves) that we
are in danger of perverting and losing the munificent
blessings Providence has conferred upon us. There
is, I fear, but too much occasion for this warning.
The pulpit should be very slow to give countenance
or currency to topics calculated to excite or alarm the
public mind; but where the UNION itself is in jeopardy,
both patriotism and religion forbid that it should remain silent. In the judgment of discreet and upright
men of all parties, a crisis of this kind has now arrived.
And, indeed, the indications of it are so palpable that
he only who shuts his eyes can fail to see them.

Up to a period quite within the recollection of the
young men before me, the atrocious word, Disunion,
was never uttered in any part of the Republic but
with abhorrence. The universal sentiment was that
the Union of these States was to be maintained at all
hazards—that it was not a question to be discussed—
and that any individual who should presume to im-
pugn its sacred obligation would be justly chargeable
with moral treason, and ought to be regarded as an
enemy to his country. This wholesome public sentiment has been for several years past gradually giving
way. Our ears have become familiarized to the word,
Disunion. A protracted session of Congress has been
consumed in discussing the thing itself. One State is
at this moment almost on the verge of secession.
Others are threatening it. And a large and vigilant

party elsewhere are pressing favorite measures with the full conviction that, if they succeed in carrying them, the Union must and will be riven asunder. Under these circumstances, the pulpit may no more keep silence than the press. We have the same civil rights as other citizens; and we do not mean lightly to surrender them. But aside from this, the interests of religion in this country are in some sort confided to the keeping of the Ministry: and Christianity—not Christianity for our own land merely, but for the world, and for all coming generations of mankind—has so much at stake in the American Union, that, if we should refuse to co-operate with our fellow-citizens in all legitimate measures for the preservation of that Union, we should be recreant to the Master we profess to serve, and unfit to minister at his altar.

In the original manuscript of Washington's Farewell Address, there is the following paragraph partially erased. With the exception of the last sentence, it was rejected by him; but no apology will be needed for citing it on an occasion like the present: "Besides the more serious causes already hinted as threatening our Union, there is one less dangerous, but sufficiently dangerous to make it prudent to be on our guard against it. I allude to the petulance of party differences of opinion. It is not uncommon to hear the irritations which these excite, vent themselves in declarations that the different parts of the United States are ill affected to each other, in menaces that the Union will be dissolved by this, or that measure.

Intimations like these are as indiscreet as they are intemperate. Though frequently made with levity, and without any really evil intention, they have a tendency to produce the consequence which they indicate. They teach the minds of men to consider the Union as precarious; as an object to which they ought not to attach their hopes and fortunes; and thus chill the sentiment in its favor. By alarming the pride of those to whom they are addressed, they set ingenuity at work to depreciate the value of the thing, and to discover reasons of indifference towards it. This is not wise.—It will be much wiser to habituate ourselves to reverence the Union as the Palladium of our National happiness; to accommodate constantly our words and actions to that idea, and to discountenance whatever may suggest a suspicion that it can in any event be abandoned."

It may be doubted whether this paragraph would not have been retained, could Washington have foreseen the events which are passing before our eyes. For there is a tone of remark now prevalent on this subject which indicates a wide-spread and perhaps growing disposition to calculate the value of the Union. That such a problem should in any quarter be seriously entertained—that it should not, on being propounded, be as summarily and indignantly thrust away as the question would be, whether we shall not replace our present form of government with a monarchy—is symptomatic of a decay of that pure and lofty patriotism which once throbbed in every Ame-

rican breast. Certain it is that those who can degrade
a theme like this to the computations of a mere commercial arithmetic, and resolve the value of the Union
as they would adjust a marine venture, or the cost of
a cotton-mill, have never even begun to comprehend
the extraordinary chain of events which led to the
establishment of this Union, the gigantic difficulties
which opposed its formation, the manifold blessings
which have resulted from it, and the legionary evils
which would be produced by its destruction. A proper discussion of these several topics in a temperate
and able manner might well engage the leisure of
some one of our eminent statesmen at the present
juncture, and could not fail to have a salutary influence on the nation at large. I propose simply to
recall your attention to THE ORIGIN OF THE UNION, AND
SOME OF THE MORE OBVIOUS CONSEQUENCES WHICH WOULD
BE LIKELY TO FLOW FROM ITS DISSOLUTION—that we may
the better understand what it is that certain parties
are proposing to accomplish.

The observation has been often made, that the
whole current of events connected with the settle-
ment of America, and the growth of the Colonies, re-
veals a purpose on the part of Divine Providence to
found, in this Western Hemisphere, a model government. They were no ordinary men who were sent
here to lay the foundations of an empire in a wilderness tenanted by wild beasts and savages. No nation
can boast a more honorable ancestry than that which

comprises the Puritans, the Huguenots, and the Quakers, who fled to this continent, that they might enjoy

"Freedom to worship God."

The seeding of the soil gave promise of a rare and generous harvest; and amply was the pledge redeemed. They knew not the exalted mission entrusted to them; it was impossible, without the gift of foresight, that they should have known it. But it is easy for us to see that, during the entire period of their colonial state, they were preparing for the work before them. In their privations and dangers, their sicknesses and wars, their mutual rivalries and quarrels; in the unnatural neglect and flagrant oppression with which they were treated by the parent government; in the sagacity, enterprise, firmness, and courage which their circumstances helped to develop; and in the continual accession to their numbers of men of kindred principles, who were driven from the old world by persecution or tyranny—we can detect a superhuman agency, which was moulding and strengthening them for the scenes of the Revolution, and the responsibilities involved in its successful termination. These, it is important to remember, demanded a training no less peculiar than the Revolution itself. It is too commonly taken for granted that, with the Peace of '83, all danger was over; that the auspicious issue of our contest with the mother country was tantamount to the creation of a free and powerful Republic. In a word, that, as soon as their battles were ended, and the chains of their colonial vassalage broken, our fathers had but to sit down in quiet and enjoy the benign protection of that glorious Union which has, under Providence, made us the most prosperous nation on the globe. This is not only an utter misconception of the facts in the case; but it is adapted to disparage the wisdom and patriotism of the men of the Revolution, and to impair our reverence for the Union itself. It is scarcely going beyond the truth to say that their work was but half accomplished with the close of their last campaign. They had severed their allegiance to the crown; but they had no adequate government of their own, and they were in a situation most unfavorable for the establishment of one. The Union, that is, such a Union as their necessities demanded, was so far from evolving itself spontaneously from the chaos which succeeded the war, that the wisest and best men among them entertained the most anxious apprehensions as to the possibility of effecting it at all. "It may be in me," said one of them,* a man whose comprehensive and penetrating intellect resolved the abstrusest theorems in political science as by intuition, and who could express his profound and luminous views in a style which would scarcely suffer by a comparison with that of Junius—"It may be in me a defect of political fortitude, but I acknowledge that I cannot entertain an equal tranquillity with those who affect to treat the dangers of a longer continu-

* Mr. Hamilton.

ance in our present situation as imaginary. A nation without a national Government is an awful spectacle. The establishment of a Constitution in time of profound peace, by the voluntary consent of a whole people, is a PRODIGY, to the completion of which I look forward with trembling anxiety. I dread the more the consequences of new attempts, because I know that powerful individuals in this State [New York] and other States, are enemies to a general national Government in every possible shape."

In a similar strain, General Washington, at an earlier period, two years after the Treaty of Peace, wrote to Mr. Jay : "What astonishing changes a few years are capable of producing! I am told that even respectable characters speak of a monarchical form of government without horror. From thinking proceeds speaking : thence to acting is often but a single step. But how irrevocable and tremendous! What a triumph for our enemies, to verify their predictions! What a triumph for the advocates of despotism, to find that we are incapable of governing ourselves, and that systems founded on the basis of equal liberty are merely ideal and fallacious! Would to God that wise measures may be taken in time to avert the consequences we have but too much reason to apprehend!"

The old Confederation would have been too weak even for the purposes of war in any other hands than those of the pure and able men who were called to conduct the Revolution. And when the outward pressure was removed, and the colonies fell back under the sway of their several local usages and interests, the compact which united them proved to be but a rope of sand. The condition of the country waxed worse and worse, until it seemed to be on the verge of some terrible catastrophe. The war had dried up its resources. The government was encumbered with a debt which it had no means of paying. Commerce was at the lowest point of declension. The colonies, oppressed by their necessities, and more solicitous to retrieve their own fortunes than those of the Union, refused the supplies of money which were indispensable to the efficiency of the Confederation, and even to its prolonged existence. The Government was the very picture of imbecility; without troops, without a revenue, without credit, without power to enforce its laws at home, or to inspire respect abroad. And the reciprocal jealousies of the colonies, reviving with the return of peace, afforded little ground to hope that any scheme of union could be devised in which they would all, or even a major part of them, coalesce. The defects of the existing league were too palpable to be denied; but the most discordant opinions prevailed as to the appropriate remedy. This may be seen in the multiform objections which were made to the new Constitution when it came to be submitted to the States for their adoption. Not to speak of the monarchical party alluded to by General Washington, and which was probably very small, the following may be taken as a sample of these objections—"This one tells us that the Constitution ought to be rejected, because it is not a Confederation of the States, but a government over individuals. Another admits that it ought to be a government over individuals to a certain extent, but not to the extent proposed. A third objects to the want of a bill of rights. A fourth would have a bill of rights, but would have it declaratory not of the personal rights of individuals, but of the rights reserved to the States in their political capacity. A fifth thinks the plan would be unexceptionable but for the fatal power of regulating the times and places of election. An objector in a large State exclaims loudly against the unreasonable equality of representation in the Senate. An objector in a small State is equally loud against the dangerous inequality in the House of Representatives. From one quarter the amazing expense of administering the new government is urged; from another the cry is that the Congress will be but a shadow of a representation, and that the government would be far less objectionable if the number and the expense were doubled. A patriot in a State that does not import discerns insuperable objections against the power of direct taxation. The patriotic adversary in a State of great exports and imports is not less dissatisfied that the whole burthen of taxes may be thrown on consumption. This politician discovers in the Constitution a direct and irresistible tendency to monarchy; *that* is equally sure it will end in aristocracy."* But it would be wearisome to

* Mr. Madison.

go on with this catalogue, and cite the objections urged against the instrument as a whole, and those advanced against the specific provisions appertaining severally to the legislative, the judicial, and the executive departments. Enough has been said to show that the convention which assembled to frame a Constitution had an herculean task to perform; and that, without the special illumination of Divine Providence, they must have essayed in vain to frame an instrument which should unite in its support the suffrages of a majority of the States.

It is an additional consideration of great weight, bearing upon this point, that they were without a model. There was no existing government which they were willing to copy. There was no government of antiquity which would at all answer their purpose. They were, in truth, not only in advance of their own age, but of all ages, in their ideas of civil government. We may apply to them what Milton has said of the Hebrew prophets: they appear

"As men divinely taught, and better teaching
The solid rules of civil government,
In their majestic, unaffected style,
Than all the oratory of Greece and Rome:
In them is plainest taught and easiest learnt,
What makes a nation happy, and keeps it so."

The concise instrument drawn up and signed in the cabin of the May Flower, was the charter of an embryo *Commonwealth*. It recognizes the great principle of equality, and the right and duty of the " civil body politic," into which the signers organized themselves, to " enact, constitute, and frame such just and equal laws, ordinances, acts, constitutions, and offices, as should be thought most convenient for the general good of the colony." This germ expanded. It derived nurture from the alternate indifference and tyranny of the home government. The colonists, not of Massachusetts only, but of Virginia and the other provinces, were compelled to act for themselves. They came to regard the "*general good,*" not the honor of a throne, or the aggrandizement of an aristocracy, as the proper end of government; and "*just and equal laws,*" as the legitimate means by which this end was to be promoted. Long before their difficulties with the crown reached their crisis, these ideas had become as familiar to their minds as household words. They were very unlike the prevailing ideas in the Old World. They found no place in the constitutions of the most liberal monarchies. Political equality—popular suffrage—equal laws—the right of the majority to govern—the greatest good of the greatest number as the end of government,—these were principles which, however they might be entertained by individuals, had yet for the first time to be *enacted*, or even recognized by any European monarchy. And when with these principles is combined another of no less importance, that of a representative republic, we shall search in vain for any adequate exposition of their views even among the so-called republics of ancient or modern times. It shows an extraordinary elevation of mind, and a moral courage stamped

with true sublimity, that they should have succeeded in divesting themselves of the intolerable
thraldom of precedent and authority, and dared to
lay the foundations of their new structure on principles which no other government had made trial of,
or which had certainly never been tested in such
combinations as were now contemplated. These
principles alone, however, were suited to the emer-
gency, and they applied them with a trustful fortitude
and a profound wisdom which have never ceased
(unless they have *now* ceased) to elicit the gratitude
of their posterity, and the admiration of enlightened
and liberal statesmen in all lands.

Without stopping to illustrate these points in detail,
let us advert for a moment to that great principle of
a representative republic which they invoked to har-
monize the conflicting rights and interests of the colonies. Our minds are so familiar with this principle
that we are scarcely in a position to appreciate the
wisdom which guided the convention to the discovery
of it (for it was a discovery), and led them to adopt
it as the core of the new Constitution. They were to
create a Government or Governments for the colonies.
Putting monarchy out of the question, these plans
were before them : 1st. Consolidation ; the dissolution
of the thirteen Provincial or State Governments, and
a general amalgamation under one republican charter. 2dly. Consolidation in the form of a pure
democracy. 3dly. The organization of thirteen entirely independent Governments—republican or demo-

cratic. 4thly. A simple Confederation of thirteen sovereignties.

These were the only models to be found in the annals of the world. All Governments not monarchical had conformed to one or another of these types: and yet the statesmen of the Revolution had the sagacity to see that they were alike either impracticable or utterly insufficient for their purposes. Consolidation was out of the question; the colonies would not consent to merge their individual existence in a single organization. A pure democracy was impracticable even for the States as such. A democracy requires the periodical convocation of the entire body of the citizens, to conduct its legislation, and is of course admissible only in the case of States comprising a very limited territory. This was a favorite scheme of a party after the war; and to elude the difficulty just stated, they were for dividing the larger colonies into districts of a tractable size. The creation of thirteen isolated sovereignties would have been the sure precursor and occasion of dissensions and wars. Nor would a simple Confederation of such a cluster of sovereignties, the scheme which was advocated by many of the most patriotic and influential men of the nation, have been essentially better. Such a Confederation already existed. Its inadequacy was matter of experience. No modification would be of any avail which came short of curing its radical vice, to wit, that of providing " legislation for States or Governments in their corporate or collective capacities, and as contradistin-

guished from the individuals of whom they consist."
So long as this principle was retained, the States might
be bound together in a league, but there could be no
national Union. Nor would a general government
be able to enforce its decrees at home or to protect
its foreign interests, if the execution of its mandates
were made contingent upon the legislation of other
independent sovereignties.* A new principle was,
therefore, needed to meet the exigencies of the case;
and it was found in that of a representative republic.
The sovereignty of the several States was left unim-
paired in respect to all matters of local jurisdiction,
while the Federal Government, springing no less
directly than the State governments from the bosom
of the people, and operating no less directly upon the
people, was clothed with the functions requisite for
the efficient administration of all interests appertaining
to the general welfare of the Republic. Thus was
the great problem solved. From the confusion and
distraction, the imbecility and exhaustion, the conflicting theories and rivalries, of these emancipated
provinces, emerged the UNION, clothed with majesty
and honor, radiant with celestial beauty, her temples
bound with a perennial olive-wreath, and her hands
filled with such blessings for the expectant people as
no nation but God's chosen one had ever dreamed of.
Tyrants looked upon her and gnashed their teeth
with rage. The patriots of every land hailed her

---

* See these points argued in the Federalist.

advent as the rising of a second sun in the heavens.
The down-trodden nations of Europe found life and
hope even in her far-off smile. And as her magic
influence penetrated their dungeons, the martyrs of
liberty felt their chains lightened, and blessed God
that, although their efforts had failed, one nation had
at length established its freedom. It was in truth
the triumph, the first great triumph, of Constitutional Liberty. The records of mankind supplied
no parallel to it; and it was a fitting occasion for a
jubilee among the friends of human progress of every
creed and country.

This cursory glance at the difficulties which were
surmounted in the formation of our government may
serve to enhance our appreciation of the Union, and
to invigorate our gratitude to the men who founded it.
A nobler race of men, or one who have a stronger
claim upon the affectionate veneration of mankind,
the world has never seen. It is impossible that they
should be forgotten so long as integrity, patriotism,
and public virtue, have a being among men. Their
names (to borrow the sublime tribute of Daniel Webster to John Hancock—a tribute which we may even
now appropriate to the great orator himself) have
a place as bright and glorious in the admiration
of mankind, " as if they had been written in letters
of light on the blue arch of heaven, between Orion
and the Pleiades." Certain it is that if *we* ever cease to
do them honor or to cherish the work of their hands,
we shall deserve the execration of all future genera-

tions. For, whatever specious objections may have
been urged against the Constitution at the period of
its adoption, it is not with us an open question
whether that immortal instrument was framed with
all the wisdom which has been claimed for it, and
whether it is adequate to the purposes for which it
was designed. The seal of more than sixty years is
now upon it, and its results are known and read of
all men. In the crypt of St. Paul's Cathedral, in
London, is the tomb of Sir Christopher Wren, the
architect of that noble structure, and the felicitous
inscription upon it runs thus : " *Reader, if you seek his
monument, look around!*" So we may say of our Constitution. If you would estimate its value, LOOK AROUND !

> " How many States,
> And clustering towns, and monuments of fame,
> And scenes of glorious deeds."

Contrast the thirteen colonies of the Revolution
with our thirty-one States. And then contrast the
Republic as a whole with any other, even the most
prosperous, empires of the globe. I give utterance
only to one of our familiar common-places, when I
say, that whether we regard the increase of its population, the development of its resources, the augmen-
tation of its wealth, its power, and its influence among
the nations, or the steady progress of its people in all
the arts of a refined civilization, the history of this
country is unexampled in the annals of our race.
Without wishing to chime in with that strain of self-
complacent declamation which has made so many

3

Fourth of July orations an offence to cultivated ears,
the occasion not only authorizes but compels me to
say, that there is no people on the earth so free as we
are; none who possess such an affluence of all the immunities and appliances, social and political, secular
and religious, essential to the plenary enjoyment of all
personal rights, and to the greatest good of the great
mass of the nation. To prove this would be a work
of supererogation. If any man can "look around"
and doubt it, he has mistaken his country, and should
transfer his domicil to a more congenial clime.

Nor is the extraordinary growth of the United
States in all the elements which constitute the true
greatness and glory of a nation more indisputable
than is the fact that we have been steadily opposed
by most of the leading cabinets of Europe, and especially by the whole moral influence of the British Government and aristocracy. England has never for-
given us the Declaration of Independence. Whether
it is because this Union is a standing memento of her
folly and misgovernment, or because she is jealous of
a daughter whose ships and spindles compete with her
own in the markets of the globe, certain it is that
she has always looked upon us with an evil eye. No
maternal pride has ever betrayed her into a spontane-
ous burst of admiration at the enterprise, the intel-
ligence, and the moral worth of her transatlantic
offspring. When James the Second, one of her faith-
less kings, whom she drove in indignation from his
throne, overlooked from the French coast the great

naval action of La Hogue, and saw the British, after
putting to flight that imposing squadron with which
all his hopes were embarked, pursue their enemy
in boats into the very shallows, and set fire to
the ships which would otherwise have escaped, he
could not restrain his admiration of their gallantry,
but cried out, "Ah, none but my brave English could
do this!" But no such paroxysm of generosity has
ever overcome our venerable mother in contemplating
this fair country. Instead of exclaiming, as she has
marked the gradual transition of this vast wilderness
into a cultivated continent, covered with towns and
cities, and smiling harvests, "None but my brave
children could have done this!" she has systemati-
cally detracted from our just fame, and disparaged
our achievements. Allowing for individual excep-
tions, the tone of her press (not to speak of other
indices of her feeling) has been marked with an
illiberality and acerbity towards us which nothing
could justify. Her journalists and tourists have set
themselves to misrepresent and depreciate our institutions. From her stately Quarterlies down to the
humblest hebdomadal repositories of provincial wit and
wisdom, they have exerted their ten talents or their one
talent, as the case might be, to cast ridicule upon our
public acts and monuments, upon our civil franchises,
our manners, our literature, our very roads and
vehicles, and the whole working of our political and
social systems. They have done what they could to
make the impression in Europe that our great " ex-

periment" was a failure; that there was no security here for life and property; that anarchy and semi-barbarism were already rampant; and that the Union must presently fall to pieces. And how has the country heeded these unworthy demonstrations? Precisely as a loaded train heeds the straws which sportive children scatter on the rails; or as an eagle heeds the pellets of mud cast after him as he soars upwards on his mighty pinions towards the sun. The country has advanced with a constantly accelerated momentum, which has at least changed the contempt of its maligners into the dignity of hatred. And neither defamatory presses nor official decrees, neither standing armies nor a domiciliary espionage, nor all these combined, have been able to conceal the truth from the simple-minded peasantry and the degraded operatives of Europe. Alike in their pestiferous work-shops and in their remote mountain *chalets,* the name of the United States is a talisman to them. The salutation, "I am an *American* citizen," is the best passport a stranger can have to their confidence. Often have I seen their eyes sparkle on hearing it; and the sight made me proud of my country. It was the boast of the ancient Roman that the watch-word, "I am a Roman citizen," would secure him personal respect throughout the known world. But it was the dread of the imperial eagles which insured his safety. No such sentiment protects the American abroad. It is not the inspiration of fear, but of love, which lights up the countenances of the common

people at his approach. They know little of politics,
and less of geography. They have read but few
books. They could give no very lucid account of this
country. But they have these two ideas about it
inwrought into their minds, viz., that it is a free country, and that the people are comfortable and con-
tented. This makes it a land of hope to them. This
makes them long to get here. This constitutes the
subtle, mysterious influence which has gone out from
our Union into all the hamlets and all the mines and
forges of Europe; and which is drawing their tenantry
towards us with an agency as irresistible as that
which keeps the needle to the pole. This it was
which made an honest, truthful peasant, who lived in
one of those lofty valleys at the base of Mont Blanc,
say to a party of Americans, a year or two since:
"Not less than two hundred of my neighbors have
gone from this small valley to your country, and
nothing but the want of means keeps me from following them." I say again, I was proud to hear it.
These unbought testimonies to the all-pervading and
blessed influence of my country—testimonies picked
up by the wayside, and by the cotter's hearth, and
the shepherd's fold, from reapers, and wagoners, and
guides, and laborers—are worth more than all the
studied compliments ever bestowed upon America by
courtly diplomatists. It is something to belong to a
land which looms up in this way before all nations,
as a land of peace and plenty, of virtue and safety—
as an asylum where the oppressed may find a refuge

from tyranny, and the poor the amplest scope and encouragement for frugal industry. It is something to belong to a land which is known wherever the foot of civilized man has trod, not by her Cæsars and Napoleons, not by her bloody wars and conquests, but by her Washingtons and Franklins, her civil and religious liberty, her equal laws, and her thriving populations. That such a land should *draw* upon the Old World is not surprising. The philosophy of the fact is sufficiently simple, and it was set forth by one of the illustrious orators of the Revolution with a felicity which is equalled only by his extraordinary prophetic announcement of the fact itself. Immediately after the close of the Revolution, Patrick Henry delivered a speech of great power in the Assembly of Virginia in favor of a liberal policy on the subject of immigration. Contrasting the expanse of our territory with the scanty population, he observed, " Your great want, sir, is the want of men, and these you must have, and will have speedily, if you are wise. Do you ask, how are you to get them? Open your doors, sir, and they will come in; the population of the Old World is full to overflowing; that population is ground, too, by the oppressions of the governments under which they live. Sir, they are already standing on tip-toe upon their native shores, and looking to your coasts with a wishful and longing eye; they see here a land blessed with natural and political advantages, which are not equalled by those of any other country upon earth; a land on which a gracious

Providence hath emptied the horn of abundance; a
land over which Peace hath now stretched forth her
white wings, and where Content and Plenty lie down
at every door! Sir, they see something still more
attractive than all this; they see a land in which
Liberty hath taken up her abode; that Liberty whom
they had considered as a fabled goddess, existing only
in the fancies of poets; they see her here a real
divinity, her altars rising on every hand throughout
these happy States, her glories chanted by three millions of tongues, and the whole region smiling under
her blessed influence. Sir, let but this celestial goddess, Liberty, stretch forth her fair hand toward the
people of the Old World, tell them to come, and bid
them welcome; and you will see them pouring in
from the north, from the south, from the east, and
from the west; your wilderness will be cleared and
settled, your deserts will smile, your ranks will be
filled; and you will soon be in a condition to defy the
powers of any adversary." Liberty did "stretch forth
her hand towards the Old World," and this eloquent
prophecy glided into history. The three millions
who chanted her glories have now become twenty-
five millions; and the mighty current of humanity is
setting towards our shores with a depth and a majesty
which are enough to awe every thoughtful beholder.
There are various aspects, economical, political, and
religious, in which this imposing movement may be
viewed. The twofold object for which it is cited
here is to illustrate, on the one hand, the unprece-

dented growth of our country; and, on the other, the
Antæan hold which this Union has taken upon the
other hemisphere. Without restricting the remark
to this wonderful migration from the Old World to the
New, we are safe in affirming that the sublime spectacle of a self-governed and well-governed nation has
told with prodigious effect upon the dynasties of Europe. For "the greatest engine of moral power
known to human affairs is an organized, prosperous
State. All that man in his individual capacity can
do—all that he can effect by his private fraternities,
by his ingenious discoveries and wonders of art, or by
his influence over others—is as nothing, compared
with the collective, perpetuated influence on human
affairs and human happiness of a well-constituted,
powerful commonwealth. It blesses generations with
its sweet influence. Even the barren earth seems to
pour out its fruits under a system where rights and
property are secure; whilst her fairest gardens are
blighted by despotism."* Such an example has been
before the world for more than half a century; and
while it is impossible to trace the influences which
have gone out from it upon the other hemisphere, all
parties are agreed that it has had a most effective
agency in bringing about the ameliorating changes
which have taken place in the European Governments. The reforms in those governments, which
have consisted essentially in raising the people from a

* Mr. Edward Everett.

condition of political nonentity to a substantive power
in the State, have drawn their animating breath and
derived their most effective support from the precedent supplied by these United States. If the Nessel-
rodes and Metternichs of the day are competent
witnesses, this country has been the great laboratory
from whence "liberal ideas" have been continually
flitting across the ocean and disturbing the Dead Sea
tranquillity of the venerable despotisms of Europe.
The extent to which these ideas have permeated the
masses there is really surprising, when one considers
the vigilance and severity with which tyranny every-
where guards its usurpations. Many a generous
struggle has proved abortive, and hecatombs of brave
but unfortunate patriots have been immolated to the
Moloch of absolutism; but the cause of freedom has
on the whole advanced. The nations are not where
they were at the commencement of this century; and
unless we betray *our* trust, and extinguish the light
which now allures them on to freedom, there is little
likelihood that they will ever consent to resume their
chains. If we guard this vestal flame upon which so
many anxious eyes are turned, the political renova-
tion of the world must go on. Other lands will be
emancipated, and the prophetic vision so beautifully
depicted by the poet will be realized :—

> " I saw the expecting regions stand,
> To catch the coming flame in turn ;
> I saw from ready hand to hand
> The bright but struggling glory burn.

And each, as she received the flame,
  Lighted her altar with its ray;
Then, smiling to the next who came,
  Speeded it on its sparkling way."*

No man who believes that there is a Providence
can take even a brief retrospect of our history, like
that which has now engaged our attention, without discovering innumerable evidences of his benignant agency. He who does not see a Divine hand
directing and controlling the whole course of our
affairs, from the landing of the colonists at James-
town and Plymouth until the present hour, would
hardly have seen the pillar of cloud and of fire had
he been with the Hebrews in the wilderness. This
Union is not the work of man. It is THE WORK OF GOD.
Among the achievements of his wisdom and benefi-
cence in conducting the secular concerns of the world,
it must be ranked as one of his greatest and best
works. And he who would destroy it is chargeable
with the impiety of attempting to subvert a structure
which is eminently adapted to illustrate the perfec-
tions of the Deity, and to bless the whole family of
man.

There are, however—the fact cannot be disguised—
parties actually at work in endeavoring to destroy
the Union. A party at the South and another party
at the North, the poles apart in their speculative

---

* I am indebted to Mr. Everett for this beautiful quotation.

views of the subject which agitates them, and inflamed
with a bitter mutual hostility, have virtually joined
hands for the purpose of demolishing this Government. This is not, indeed, as to one of these parties,
the ostensible object they have in view; but it is
essentially involved in that object, and they know it.
They must, therefore, be held to the responsibility of
aiming at a dissolution of the Union, equally with
those inhabitants of the Southern States who avow
this as their aim.

The subject which has occasioned this commotion
is SLAVERY. The Southern Disunionists would secede
because Congress, at its late session, passed certain
acts abridging, as they allege, the rights of the slave-
holding States; and the Northern Disunionists insist
upon the repeal of a law passed at the same time,
entitled the Fugitive Slave Law, even though its
abrogation should involve a dissolution of the Union.
My business as a Northern man, and a citizen of a
free State, is with the latter of these parties, or rather
with the North generally. In the few observations
I am about to make on the subject, I shall simply
reiterate sentiments which have been so often and so
eloquently expressed both in Congress and out of it,
that they have become familiar to every well-informed
citizen. But I may say that the man who can put
the American Union, with all its untold and incon-
ceivable blessings, into one scale, and the repeal of
the Fugitive Slave Law into the other, and then
strike the balance in favor of the latter, is without an

exemplar in the history of the race until we get back
to the record of that primeval tempter who said to
our first mother, " Ye shall not surely die."

> " She pluck'd, she eat !
> Earth felt the wound, and Nature from her seat,
> Sighing thro' all her works, gave signs of woe,
> That all was lost !"

In saying this, I utterly disclaim any design to become the champion of Slavery. I have never set my-
self to defend it; and by the grace of God I never will.
I concur in the estimate which is put upon it by the
people of the North, and by tens of thousands of our
Southern countrymen, that it is a colossal evil; and
that no consummation is more devoutly to be wished
and prayed for than its removal. But I can as little
undertake the championship of Northern agitators
and fanatics as that of Slavery. I believe they are
the worst enemies of the slave, and the most efficient
protectors of Slavery; and as such, I can have no
fellowship with them. The law to which they object
may be, or it may not be, defective or unjust in some
of its provisions. If it is, it will no doubt at the
proper time be amended; if it is not, it will stand.
But what we are called upon to discountenance is
the spirit in which this excitement is promoted—the
recklessness and violence with which the unconditional repeal of the obnoxious law is demanded, irre-
spective of consequences—the abusive attacks which
are constantly made upon the South—and the whole
system of measures put in operation to alienate the

two portions of the confederacy, and bring about a
disruption.

However the fact may be contemned by the radical
Abolitionists, it behooves us all to remember, what
even the cursory retrospect presented in this discourse
must have made sufficiently manifest, that the Union
of these States was a matter of compromise. Ob-
structed as it was by the most serious impediments, it
could never have been effected had not all the parties
concerned been animated by a rare spirit of accom-
modation. General Washington, in submitting the
draft of the new Constitution to Congress, thus ex-
presses himself in his official letter as the President of
the Convention : " In all our deliberations on this
subject, we kept steadily in our view that which ap-
pears to us the greatest interest of every true American, the consolidation of our Union, in which is
involved our prosperity, felicity, safety, perhaps our
national existence. This important consideration,
seriously and deeply impressed on our minds, led
each State in the Convention to be less rigid on points
of inferior magnitude than might have been otherwise expected; and thus the Constitution which we
now present is the result of a spirit of amity, and of
that mutual deference and concession which the pecu-
liarity of our political situation rendered indispensable."

In this spirit the Union originated, and in this
spirit it has, under God's blessing, been preserved.
On all the most important measures of the government,

the country has been divided into two great parties.
We have passed through various crises, which have
tested the loyalty of one party or of the other, as
the case might be, as in a fiery furnace. Take for
example the following measures : Jay's Treaty—the
Embargo—the War of 1812—the Missouri question—
the Nullification controversy—the admission of Texas
—and the Mexican War. Each of these measures was
highly offensive to a large portion of the American
people. The legislation of Congress was, in some of
the cases, resisted by Statesmen of the most eminent
abilities, as being in the face of the Constitution and
destructive to our best interests. But when the acts
were passed, the law-abiding spirit of the Anglo-Saxon
race began to work, and all parties acquiesced. We
have a striking illustration of this in one of the most
recent of the measures just mentioned, the admission
of Texas. The major part of the population in the
free States regarded this, in the manner in which it
was done, as a gross invasion of the Constitution. A
distinguished citizen of South Carolina, formerly Go-
vernor of that State, has remarked, in a letter recently
published, that "the admission of Texas furnished a
far greater provocation to the North to secede, than
the admission of California does to the South, with
the auxiliary stipulations incident to the former."*
But we did not secede. Nobody talked of seceding,
except the party who are driving at disunion now.

* General James Hamilton's Letter to the People of South Carolina.

The sober sense and enlightened patriotism of the mass
of the people, fortified by sixty years' experience, have
taught them the necessity of forbearance, and made
them feel that it is far better to submit even to what
they believe to be wrong and hurtful measures than to
break up the Union. They have no notion of setting
the ship on fire because the captain deals out some
oppressive orders. They choose rather to wait till
the ship returns to port, and then, if they can, get a
new captain.—In this spirit the compromise measures
of the last session ought to be treated. They were
not party measures, for none of the recognized parties
was, as such, satisfied with them. But they supplied
the only platform on which men of all parties could
meet; and this is a sufficient reason why the country
should acquiesce in them.

That a statute respecting fugitive slaves should form
a part of this series of pacificatory measures, was a
thing of course. One of the chief compromises of the
Constitution itself relates to this very subject. The
South would not come into the Union without some
guarantee on this point, and the following section
(Art. IV. Sect. 2) was adopted by the Convention—
I believe unanimously. "No person held to service
or labor in one State, under the laws thereof, escap-
ing into another, shall, in consequence of any law or
regulation therein, be discharged from such service or
labor, but shall be delivered up on claim of the party
to whom such service or labor may be due." A law
was enacted under Washington's administration, and

with his approval, to carry this provision of the Constitution into effect.* This law had of late years
been rendered nugatory in some of the States by local
legislation, and it became necessary to replace it with
another. This is the statute which is now exciting
so much opposition, and the execution of which has
been resisted with so much violence. These demonstrations, although professedly directed against some
of the details of the act, are to a great extent levelled
against its principle. We do the party concerned in
them no injustice in supposing that they would be
equally hostile to any adequate law designed to effect
the same object. In this view, one cannot but be
struck with the flexible morality which can declaim
fiercely about the inalienable rights of man, while it
is trampling under its feet one of the most sacred
covenants which ever bound a people together. There
is no difference of opinion as to the meaning of the
Constitutional provision on this subject. To that

---

* It must be recorded, to the lasting honor of Pennsylvania, that she
was the first of the thirteen States to abolish Slavery. This was done
under the administration of President Reed, in 1780. And it is a cir-
cumstance worthy of note, that the act embraces a provision for the
extradition of fugitive slaves. The following is an extract from its
Eleventh Section: "Provided always, and be it further enacted, that
this act, or anything in it contained, shall not give any relief or shelter
to any absconding or runaway negro, or mulatto slave or servant, who
has absented himself, or shall absent himself, from his or her owner.
master or mistress, residing in any other State or Country; but such
owner, master, or mistress, shall have like right and aid to demand.
claim, and take away his slave or servant, as he might have had in case
this act had not been made."

provision, in common with the others, our fathers assented, and we have assented. It is one of the terms of a compact into which we have as a people entered with one another; and which is just as binding upon us as any other of its provisions. Our judgment may condemn it. It may be very revolting to our feelings. But this is nothing to the purpose. We are under no obligation to remain in a country which we believe to be governed by oppressive laws; there is nothing to prevent our flying to any land which rejoices in a milder code and a more rational liberty. But as long as we continue citizens of this Union, we must abide by its Constitution and obey its laws.* And we cannot consent to take lessons in ethics from those who deny this proposition. The first requisite we demand in a teacher of morals is that he be a moral man himself. And when a covenant-breaker comes to expound to us our obligations, we feel disposed to decline his instructions and to say to him,

> "Your nickname, virtue; vice, you should have spoke;
> For virtue's office never breaks men's troth."

To some persons this may sound very unfeeling as regards the slave. I will not reply by saying that the Apostle Paul thought it no sin to send a fugitive back to his master. But this is a case where we are not at liberty to take counsel merely of our sympa-

---

* It is not necessary, for the purposes of the present argument, to state the limitations of this principle.

4

thies. The obligation of contracts is not made contingent upon men's feelings; and if this plea was to be urged at all, it should have been before the Constitution was adopted. We do not, however, rest our answer,to the objection on this ground only. We are not willing to concede a monopoly of all the sympathy which is entertained for the bondman to the party which is clamoring for an unconditional repeal of the Fugitive Slave Law. So far from it, we claim to be the truest friends of the slave. We believe that, as well for nations and in respect to public affairs, as for individuals, " Honesty is the best policy;" and that kindness to the colored race, no less than patriotism, demands a faithful adherence on the part of all concerned to the stipulations of the Constitution. By that instrument the exclusive jurisdiction of slavery is reserved to the several States. We have no more right to dictate to South Carolina what she shall do with her slaves than she has to prescribe to Pennsylvania what railroads we shall construct or what banks we shall charter. Nor does the responsibility of her system of servitude any more attach to us than does the responsibility of the serfdom of Russia. The Northern abolitionists (I use the term in its technical sense), impressed, it would seem, with a conviction that their proper responsibilities, sectional and national, secular and spiritual, are not commensurate with their capacities, have volunteered to shoulder by much the heaviest portion of the obligations resting upon the Southern States. The South declines the

proffered civility; but they press their attentions. The
South remonstrates, on the ground that the contemplated interference would be highly prejudicial to her
tranquillity; but her officious friends insist upon it as
their right to help her manage her private affairs.
The South at length puts herself in an attitude of
resistance, and points to the solemn compact in the
Constitution; but they reply, with an air of triumph,
that they are governed by a "*higher law,*" and that
under that law, it is not only their right but their
duty to take charge of her slaves. And what have
they accomplished by this Quixotic generosity? They
have riveted the fetters of the slave. They have
deterred at least three States, Maryland, Virginia, and
Kentucky, from carrying out the plans of prospective
emancipation they were just entering upon when
this outbreak of misguided philanthropy occurred at
the North. They have scattered the seeds of discord
and alienation broad-cast through the Confederacy.
In a word, protesting that they were the exclusive
friends of the slave, they have taken him to their
breasts with a hug which reminds one of the embrace
of that terrific automaton of the Virgin found in the
dungeons of the "Holy Inquisition," which, clasping
the victim in its arms and pressing him to its bosom,
transfixed him with a thousand concealed spikes and
knife-blades. And their fitting auxiliaries in all this
crusade against the South have been British emissa-
ries; the subjects of that crown which, in the face of
the remonstrances of some of the colonies, planted

slavery in our soil and fostered it into manhood, and which at this moment has millions of subjects at home and in its colonies who would be the gainers in physical comfort, and even in spiritual privilege, by exchanging places with our Southern slaves.

The failure of all past efforts at the North to ameliorate the condition of the slave is not more palpable than is the certainty that the grand expedient now contemplated would prove equally abortive. For, suppose radicalism could achieve its purpose and split the Union to pieces, *how would this help the slave?* Does any man, not a tenant of a Lunatic Asylum, believe that Disunion would mitigate the evils of Southern servitude? Would it bring about a relaxation of the laws which regulate it? Would it incline the planters to put books and pens into the hands of their slaves? Would it facilitate the flight of fugitives? Would it conciliate the various legislatures towards schemes of emancipation? No one is so infatuated as to affirm this. The most frantic abolitionists must be aware that the disruption of the Union would put a cup of gall and wormwood to the lips of every slave; that it would be a signal for the enactment of more stringent laws than have ever appeared upon the Southern Statute-books; and for the institution of a system of *surveillance* on every plantation and in every household, the rigor of which has no parallel in the records of American bondage. In the name, then, of three millions of slaves, we protest against all schemes for dissolving the Union.

We believe that, terrible as such a catastrophe would be to the whites, it would be no less so to the blacks; that it would abridge their privileges, augment their burdens, and postpone by many years the period of their ultimate emancipation. And we should be criminally indifferent to their welfare, as well as treacherous to those sacred bonds which have hitherto united the North and the South in an honorable and affectionate brotherhood, if we could remain silent when sincere but mistaken religionists and unprincipled demagogues have well nigh precipitated the country into this frightful abyss. And we are all the more disposed to break silence because we believe that, of the two classes of agitators just named, the latter has a great deal more to do with the present excitement than the former. There is, it is true, a settled conviction in the minds of the Northern people that slavery is a great evil, and there is an anxious desire to see the country rid of it. But, left to itself, this feeling is as still as it is strong and deep; and it never could have been lashed into the foaming surges which now break over the land but through the systematic, crafty, and wicked exertions of political demagogues. There were men in the ancient republics whose motto was,

" Better to reign in hell than serve in Heaven ;"

and they cared not what became of their country, so *they* were promoted. Monsters, it has been said, cannot perpetuate their species; but this species, if not perpetuated, has been reproduced, for we indubitably have

them among ourselves. Like Erostratus, who, when
put to the torture, confessed that his motive in setting
fire to the magnificent temple of Diana at Ephesus
was to gain himself a name among posterity, these
men appear to be intent upon attracting to themselves the attention of the world, even though it can
be done only by applying the torch of civil war to
this glorious Union. Let us hope that a merciful
Providence will baffle their designs; that the upright
and law-abiding people whom they have, for the time,
bewitched with their enchantments, will detect the
real character of their leaders; and that these local
ebullitions of fanaticism will soon give place to those
patriotic and conciliatory sentiments which have in
every previous crisis of our history proved equally effi-
cacious against domestic faction and foreign aggression.

It would be well for all classes of our citizens, at
this critical juncture, to look Disunion fairly in the
face. Its unavoidable effects upon the colored population constitute but a tithe of the evils which would
flow from it. Not to exhaust your patience by going
into the question at large, let it suffice to say that
Disunion not only involves a fratricidal war, but that
it would undoubtedly lead to a continued series of
contentions and disruptions among the States. It
seems to be taken for granted that, if we divide, we
divide into two confederations. But why stop at
two? It would be quite as natural certainly to form
four confederations as two. And how long should we
pause at four? A sense of common danger might

hold the new combinations together for a season; but this would give place, after a while, to local and more potent influences. The strength of the Union lies not in its physical, but its moral power. Its real buttresses are not its army and navy, its mines and factories, its canals and railroads—not even its written constitutions and charters, its laws and tribunals; but its sacred traditions, the inwrought and, until lately, universal conviction of its unparalleled benefits, and that sense of its *sanctity* which has made the nation regard it with a reverential awe akin to that with which the Hebrews looked upon the ark of the covenant. The feeling has been that the Union *was* another ark of the covenant to us—that it was the repository of our most precious national mementoes, the symbol of the Divine presence with us, and the pledge of his future protection. This feeling is not to be ascribed to any specific training. It is no set lesson we have learned at school, or which has been drilled into us like a code of morals or a code of manners at home. We have inherited it from the mothers who bore us; we have inhaled it in the air of heaven; it has gathered nourishment from the scenes of our firesides, from our daily employments, from our journeys, from our sanctuaries, from our national anniversaries, from all our experiences and all our associations. It has grown with our growth and strengthened with our strength, and imperceptibly become a part of our being. And this it is which, under God, has made the Union so strong; it is because its roots are struck down into our hearts, and so interlaced with the very framework of our moral being, that they seem to belong to our personal identity.

Now dissolve the Union, and not only do we cease to be what we have been, as individuals, but the power of the Union over us is gone, and gone forever. You annihilate by one stroke that feeling of its sanctity which has done more to preserve it than all other causes combined. And it matters not whether you merely cleave it in halves or divide it down into quarters or eighths. One pebble will spoil a mirror as well as a handful. The people will have learned, from a single rupture, that the Union is frangible—a most fatal discovery. For when they, have broken it once, they will not scruple, if occasion serves, to break it, or rather to break its fragments again; for it will have ceased to be the Union. We shall no longer have a national existence. The great events of our history—the illustrious names which adorn our annals —the heritage of renown committed to us—can no longer be appealed to as incentives to virtuous conduct, or as rallying-cries in seasons of peril. What orator will dare allude to Bunker Hill or York-town, to Champlain or Erie? What senator will dare invoke the name of Washington—or to speak of Henry and Marshall, of Greene and Morgan, of Jackson and Harrison, of Hull and Bainbridge? These illustrious men toiled and bled for the UNION; and when we shall have destroyed the work of their hands, and resolved the almost perfect government they established or defended at so great a cost into a group of petty jarring confederacies, shame will conspire with ingratitude in consigning their names, their honors, and their sufferings, to a speedy and an eternal oblivion. Nothing—if this calamity awaits us—nothing presents itself to our expectations but a future as humiliating and disastrous as our past has been bright and ennobling. Instead of that beneficent mission which we have been wont to suppose had been confided to us, of leading the nations on to freedom and happiness, we may look forward to protracted scenes of anarchy and bloodshed, which will sicken and discourage the patriots of other lands, and supply the partisans of arbitrary power with a triumphant proof that nations require a master.

We are not at liberty to disregard this consideration. Even if we were so lost to virtue and patriotism as to be reckless of the fate of our own countrymen, we could not elude the responsibilities which rest upon us in reference to the world at large. This Union cannot expire as the snow melts from the rock, or a star disappears from the firmament. When it falls, the crash will be heard in all lands. Wherever the winds of Heaven go, that will go, bearing sorrow and dismay to millions of stricken hearts. Not the dismay and sorrow incident to the blighting of their own prospects and the breaking up of their household plans; but the deep and inconsolable grief occasioned by a calamity so startling and so disastrous in its

bearings upon the happiness of mankind as to leave
the mind no opportunity for expatiating on its own
private misfortunes. For the subversion of this Government will render the cause of CONSTITUTIONAL
LIBERTY hopeless throughout the world. What nation
can govern itself, if this nation cannot? What encouragement will any people have to establish liberal institutions for themselves, if ours fail? Providence has laid
upon us the responsibility and the honor of solving that
problem in which all coming generations of men have a
profound interest, whether the true ends of government
can be secured by a popular representative system.
In the munificence of his goodness, he put us in pos-
session of our heritage by a series of interpositions
scarcely less signal than those which conducted the
Hebrews to Canaan; and He has up to this period
withheld from us no immunities or resources which
might facilitate an auspicious result. Never before
was a people so advantageously situated for working
out this great problem in favor of human liberty.
And it is important for us to understand that the
world so regards it. The argument with which Na-
poleon inflamed the ardor of his troops on the eve of
the great battle of the Pyramids was in these preg-
nant words, " Soldiers! consider that from the sum-
mits of yonder Pyramids forty centuries look down
upon you." Whatever the rhetoricians may say of
this speech, they must at least admit that the principle to which it appeals constitutes one of the most
powerful springs of human action, and that no man

is at liberty to disregard its promptings. We, certainly, are bound to remember that the nations are
looking to us, not for themselves only, but for the
"centuries" which are to follow, to learn whether
"order and law, religion and morality, the rights of
conscience, the rights of persons, and the rights of
property, may all be preserved and secured in the
most perfect manner by a government entirely and
purely elective." And if, in the frenzy of our base
sectional jealousies, we dig the grave of the Union,
and thus decide this question in the negative, no
tongue may attempt to depict the disappointment and
despair which will go along with the announcement
as it spreads through distant lands. It will be at once
the most unlooked-for and the most irrefragable tes-
timony ever given to the odious theory, that princes
were made to govern, and nations only to obey. It
will be America, after fifty years' experience, in
the course of which period she had done more to inspire the nations with a desire for liberal institutions
than all other popular Governments combined had
effected in the lapse of ages, giving in her adhesion
to the doctrine that man was not made for self-govern-
ment. It will be Freedom herself proclaiming that
Freedom is a chimera ; Liberty ringing her own knell
all over the globe. And when the citizens or *subjects*
of the Governments which are to succeed this Union
shall visit Europe, and see in some land, now
struggling to cast off its fetters, the lacerated and
lifeless form of Liberty laid prostrate under the iron

heel of despotism, let them remember that the blow
which destroyed her was inflicted by their own country.

> " So the struck Eagle, stretched upon the plain,
> No more through rolling clouds to soar again,
> Viewed his own feather on the fatal dart,
> And winged the shaft that quivered in his heart.
> Keen were his pangs, but keener far to feel
> He nursed the pinion which impelled the steel;
> While the same plumage that had warmed his nest
> Drank the last life-drop of his bleeding breast."

Nor is this the only aspect in which the issues of
Disunion present themselves to our contemplation.
We are forced to consider them as well in respect to
our spiritual as our civil and social interests. For
the most remarkable characteristic of this whole
movement is that the sacred name of RELIGION
should be invoked to give a sanction to measures
adapted to destroy this government; the Union is to
be broken up for the sake of religion! The lofty
morality of the Scriptures will not permit us to live
together under a constitution which authorizes the
Fugitive Slave Law; and we must separate.

> "I thought where all thy circling wiles would end;
> In feign'd religion, smooth hypocrisy!"

It needed but this ingredient to consummate the su-
perlative madness and impiety of this scheme. For, if
there is any one great national interest upon which the
disruption of these States would fall with a crushing
weight, it is our CHRISTIANITY—that interest which

as much surpasses all others in importance as it will
in duration.

There is no land where Christianity has achieved
nobler victories than it has here. Enjoying at once plenary protection from the State and the utmost freedom,
it has developed itself with a purity and an energy
rarely witnessed in the Old World. It was a sublime
undertaking, that of supplying, without the aid of en-
dowments or government patronage, churches and spiritual teachers for a youthful and growing nation like
this, diffused over so great an expanse of territory.
And the predictions of failure were equally sanguine
and universal among the adherents of the ecclesias-
tical establishments of Europe. But these predictions
have not been verified. We may venture to assert,
without violating the modesty proper to the occasion,
that Christianity has accomplished far more than its
friends could have anticipated; that the efficiency of
the voluntary principle, as displayed here, has excited
the astonishment of its bitterest opponents; and that
we have done more by our example to refute the
vicious theories of foreign statesmen and ecclesiastics,
and to promote the progress of religious liberty on
that side of the water, than could have been done by
whole libraries of polemical divinity. The time forbids me to go into detail. But no candid observer
can survey our country, in its moral and religious
features, without being impressed with the grandeur
of the results already achieved here. Not to speak
of the churches with which the land is dotted

over; the large body of educated and evangelical
clergymen who occupy our pulpits and conduct most
of the higher literary institutions; the liberal sums
spontaneously contributed for the support and propa-
gation of the Gospel; and the promptitude with
which further subsidies and new laborers are supplied as fresh fields demand cultivation; look at
the benign and powerful influence religion has exerted upon the population at large. There was a
work to be done here so indispensable that the government could not get on tranquilly without it, but which
the government could not do. Religion has done it.
It has been the chief agent in establishing our systems
of education. It has been the main-spring of most of
the humane institutions designed to alleviate the
wants and improve the condition of the people. It
has gone down among the masses, and not only fed
them and clothed them, but renovated their principles, restrained their passions, taught them their
duties, and made them value their privileges. It has
received in the arms of its comprehensive charity the
myriads who land upon our wharves; and done more
by its wondrous alchemy, than all other agencies combined, to transmute them into good citizens, and to
homologate all creeds and parties and tongues in a
harmonious brotherhood. It has redoubled its exertions to keep pace with the tide of emigration as it
has rolled over the prairies, pierced the primeval
forests of the West, and poured itself down the slopes
of the Rocky Mountains upon the fertile plains of

Oregon and into the auriferous valleys of California.
And, not satisfied with domestic conquests, though
stretching from ocean to ocean, it has sent forth its
peaceful cohorts to distant shores; and from Asia,
from Africa, from the Isles of the Sea, ten thousand
voices come back to proclaim their bloodless victories,
and to assure us that the wilderness and the solitary
place have been made glad for them, and the desert
rejoices and blossoms as the rose.

Now let the Union be dissolved, and how certainly
will this vision pass away. For it is not possible that
this event should occur without involving religion in
the general catastrophe. It is a common maxim that,
in times of public distress or alarm, credit is the first
thing to suffer. It is no less true that RELIGION sym-
pathizes at such crises, not only with credit, but with
every other element of prosperity. Christianity is not
a thing by itself—a mere matter of Bible-reading and
Church-going, of Sundays and Sacraments. It is in-
terfused, as we have just seen, through all our rela-
tions, comprehends all our employments, and exerts
its prerogative over the whole field of human duty.
The moment you touch the commerce or the hus-
bandry of a country, you touch its Christianity. If you
paralyze any branch of industry, weaken the popular
confidence in the government, excite an expectation
of war, or do anything else to agitate the public
mind, religion feels the effect of it. It requires no
prophet, therefore, to foresee that, in the event of a
disruption, the churches would share in the common

fortunes of the country. Amidst despondency and
terror, dissensions and war, their strength would
dwindle and their zeal decline. With diminished resources, the money now appropriated to the mainte-
nance and diffusion of the Gospel would be wanted
to pay troops and purchase munitions of war; or,
should an appeal to arms be averted, to meet the
enormous taxes for civil and military purposes incident to the new order of things, and the critical rela-
tions among the several States and Federations. It
is no extravagant supposition that, if the process of
dissolution once begins, it will not finally stop until
the Republic is chopped up into six or eight distinct
Leagues, each one of which must have its own general
government, with the usual symbols and implements
of nationality, such as Legislative and Judicial tribunals, ambassadors, a navy, and, what will then be
unavoidable, a cordon of camps and fortresses and a
considerable standing army. The very transit from
our present condition to a state like this would be
like the passage of a fleet through the Norwegian
Maelstrom. It would extinguish hundreds of feeble
churches and shatter the strongest ones. Instead of
keeping pace with the spiritual wants of our nomadic
population, which they are barely able to do when
blessed with a redundant prosperity, the various de-
nominations would find it difficult to sustain themselves at home. Foreign Missionaries would be re-
called, and fields restored to paganism which have
been won from it at a great outlay of money and life,

and which are now "white to the harvest." The circumstances of the country would be as unpropitious to the culture of sound morals as they are now favorable. Infidelity and atheism would run riot through the land, violence and crime would superabound, and we should deteriorate in all those high moral qualities which have hitherto attested the efficacy of our Christianity and secured for us the respect of the civilized world.

And all this avalanche of evil is to be brought down upon us for the sake of RELIGION! We are to exchange our present condition for alienation, insecurity, commercial prostration, the decay of our churches, and the bankruptcy of our great charities—for the sake of religion! We are to make the Bible a nullity, and the Sabbath a day of amusement, re-open all the sluices of immorality, and deluge the land with licentiousness and profanity—for the sake of religion! We are to disband our schools and churches among the heathen, and send back the multitudes, now under Christian instruction, to worship in idol temples and sacrifice their children to devils, for the sake of religion!

We protest against this huge impiety. If fanatics and demagogues are resolved to destroy this Union, let them not pretend to sanctify the parricidal crime by perpetrating it in the name of religion. Enough that Buddhism should crush its deluded devotees under the car of Juggernaut, in the name of religion; that Mohammed should fertilize kingdoms with human blood, in the name of religion; that a spurious Chris-

5

tianity should keep its arsenals of chains and fagots
and slaughter whole tribes of unoffending peasants,
in the name of religion. Let not Satan come *hither*
also in the robes of an angel of light. Let not
the august name of religion be invoked to hallow
an enormity which would not only shroud this
land in mourning, but inflict upon religion itself the
most irreparable injury. Every consideration of
virtue not only, but of decency, forbids that Christianity should be called upon to preside at an *auto-da-
fe* of which it is itself to be the holocaust; to conse-
crate an action which would for the time arrest its
own beneficent triumphs, clothe atheistic impiety
with superhuman power, and send a thrill of sardonic
joy through those infernal legions who exult only in
the calamities of virtue and the victories of sin.

Not to pursue this painful theme, it must be too
apparent to require argument that the dismemberment of this Union would be one of the most appal-
ling calamities which could befall the world. "Other
misfortunes (I use the words of the great statesman of
Massachusetts) may be borne or their effects overcome.
If disastrous war should sweep our commerce from the
ocean, another generation may renew it; if it exhaust
our treasury, future industry may replenish it; if it
desolate and lay waste our fields, still under a new
cultivation they will grow green again and ripen to
future harvests. It were but a trifle even if the
walls of the Capitol were to crumble, if its lofty
pillars should fall, and its gorgeous decorations be all
covered by the dust of the valley. All these might

be rebuilt. But who shall reconstruct the fabric of demolished Government? Who shall rear again the well-proportioned columns of Constitutional liberty? Who shall frame together the skilful architecture which unites national sovereignty with State-rights, individual security, and public prosperity? No, if *these* columns fall, they will not be raised again. Like the Coliseum and the Parthenon, they will be destined to a mournful, a melancholy immortality. Bitterer tears, however, will flow over them than were ever shed over the monuments of Roman or Grecian art; for they will be the remnants of a more glorious edifice than Greece or Rome ever saw—the edifice of Constitutional American Liberty."* But why *should* they fall? What is it which now threatens to overwhelm this Government in irretrievable ruin? Has it become so enervated by luxury as to sink into a state of inanition? Are we falling to pieces through the extraordinary and intractable expansion of our territory? Is there a victorious army at our gates? Are we ground down with oppressive laws for which there is no remedy but in a dissolution? No: none of these. But Congress, in the exercise of a power never before called in question, has admitted a State into the Union which refused to tolerate involuntary servitude; and in obedience to an imperative requisition of the Constitution, has passed a law for the reclamation of fugitive slaves! These are the grounds on which it is proposed to destroy this Government.

---

* Mr. Webster's Speech at the celebration of Washington's Birthday, in Washington, 1832.

For *these* reasons we are called upon, in the midst of peace, plenty, and prosperity, to exchange the best Government the world has ever seen—the most affluent blessings, the most glorious reminiscences, and the most brilliant prospects a nation ever enjoyed—for dismemberment, anarchy, and carnage. Surely, if the establishment of this Union by the voluntary consent of the people was, as Mr. Hamilton declared, a " prodigy," its voluntary destruction by that same people or their degenerate descendants, for causes like these and after sixty years experience of its benefits, would be a far greater prodigy. The turpitude of such a crime has nothing in history to illustrate it. Language was not made to define it. The generation which perpetrates it will cover themselves with an infamy as deep as the abyss into which they will have plunged their country. And the patriots of all coming generations will execrate the memories of the men who betrayed the priceless heritage of Constitutional Liberty which was purchased with the blood of their fathers and placed in their hands as trustees for all mankind.

Let it be *our* aim to do what we can to avert so fearful a catastrophe. Let us cultivate a spirit of conciliation towards all portions of the Confederacy. Let us sustain the majesty of the law. Let us invoke the blessing of heaven upon our rulers. Let us, above all, be instant and earnest in commending our beloved country to the care of that benignant Providence who has brought us through so many dangers and crowned us with such unexampled prosperity.

www.ingramcontent.com/pod-product-compliance
Lightning Source LLC
Chambersburg PA
CBHW021639270326
41931CB00008B/1087